My Pet's Baby Book

Bill Hastings

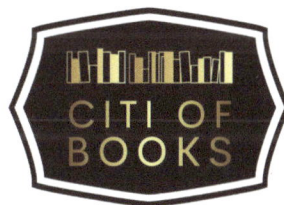

CITI OF
BOOKS

CITIOFBOOKS, INC.
3736 Eubank NE Suite A1
Albuquerque, NM 87111-3579
www.citiofbooks.com

Hotline: 1 (877) 389-2759
Fax: 1 (505) 930-7244

Ordering Information:
Quantity sales. Special discounts are available on quantity purchases by corporations, associations, and others. For details, contact the publisher at the address above.

Printed in the United States of America.

ISBN-13:   Paperback   979-8-89391-066-7

Library of Congress Control Number: 2024907925

MY PET'S KEEPSAKES

My pet is a_____

Born_____ounces_____

Weight_____pounds_____

Length_____inches_____

Color of hair_____

Color of eyes_____

Other memories_____

My Pet's First Photograph

Identification Marks

Left Front paw   Right Front paw

Left Rear paw   Right Rear paw

The World the way it was

News Headlines

Popular Songs

Current Movies

Best Selling Books

Popular TV Shows

Fashions and Fads

VISITS TO THE VETERINARY

First checkup at age

Doctor's Instruction

Pets Reaction

Results of Other Checking

Date   Doctor's Instruction

Record of Immunization

Distemper

Rabies

Hepititus

Kennel Cough

Pet's Daily Schedule

Feeding

Sleeping

Other Activities

Weight and Height Chart

Weight at birth   pounds   ounces

Length at birth   inches

Date POUNDS AND OUNCES   inches

Early birthdays

Pet's 1st Birthday

How the birthday was Celebrated

Gifts Received

Special interest and activities

weight   height

2nd Birthday

How the birthday was Celebrated

Gifts received

Special interest and activities

weight   height

3rd Birthday

How the birthday was Celebrated

Gifts received

Special interest and activities

weight   height

4th Birthday

How the birthday was Celebrated

Gifts received

Special interest and activities

weight   height

5th Birthday

How the birthday was Celebrated

Gifts received

Special interest and activities

weight   height

Memorable Holidays

Memorable Holidays

Traveling

First Outing	Date	Place
Car Trips	Date	Place
Train	Date	Place
Plane	Date	Place
Boat	Date	Place
Other	Date	Place

Pet's other Relatives

Name	Relationship	Birth Date	Birth Place

My Pet's Pedigree

Great Grandmother

Great Grandfather

Grandmother

Grandfather

father

Great Grandmother

Great Grandfather

Grandmother

Grandfather

Mother

My pet

Firsts

My pet set out to explore World. On_____ my Pet First recognized Mother's face. My Pet first rolled over on_____and listened to commands. My Pet stopped using the carpet_____and started waiting at the door. My Pet learned how to climb stairs on_____. My Pet's first word was "_____"and was said to_____on_____

My Pets hair was first cut on_____

Pets Favorites

Toy

Stories, Verse and Songs

Food

Games

Playmates

Memorable Moments

Early Keepsakes

My Pet's First Collar

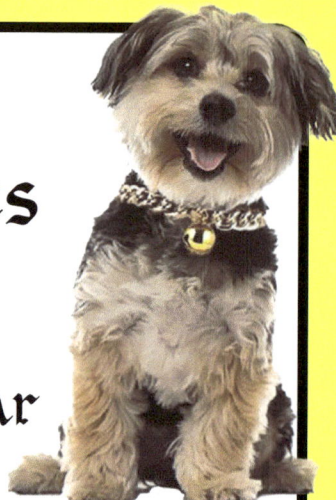

(ATTACH COLLAR HERE)

A Lock of my Pet's Hair

(ATTACH HAIR HERE)

My Pets Homecoming

Photo of my pets first home

KEEPSAKES POCKET

KEEPSAKES POCKET

Special Photos

MY PET'S KEEPSAKES